THE

"STANDUD"
GEEK
DICTIONARY

(All the computer terms you'd like to know
but were not interested enough to ask)

Stanley L. Dribble

MCSE-MCP-MCT
Microsoft Certified Systems Engineer,
Professional, and Trainer.

PublishAmerica
Baltimore

First printing

PublishAmerica has allowed this work to remain exactly as the author intended, verbatim, without editorial input.

Hardcover 978-1-4512-0126-0
Softcover 978-1-4512-0127-7
PUBLISHED BY PUBLISHAMERICA, LLLP
www.publishamerica.com
Baltimore

Printed in the United States of America

ABOUT THE AUTHOR

Stanley Louis Dribble (AKA Stan Louis), Has written many computer text books over the past 47 years while teaching computer technology in the private sector, Department of Defense, as well as State & private school systems. Some of these texts were used only in the classroom, specifically written for the curriculum of that school. Some have been published for use in the Aerospace industry as guides for manufacturing procedures and safety guidelines for space hardware. Stan Louis has also published a science fiction novel entitled "Cosmic Intelligence."

As a Microsoft Certified Systems Engineer teaching students a very complex set of programming software, hardware design, implementation, infrastructure, maintenance, troubleshooting, and repair, it can be very tedious, and at times, make it very hard to concentrate and absorb this highly technical material. To make matters worse, all the text books are written in sophisticated technical terms, which tend to confuse rather than enlighten. It would therefore make a great deal of sense to first write a book that teaches the student the terminology or the language used to express these terms.

Trying to teach people how to speak Greek by giving them a book written in the Russian language would obviously create a learning problem. Therefore a method of helping digest this information had to be found. Over the past 47 years when lectures were conducted, and humor was injected into the conversation, a very strange phenomenon took place, students actually begun to remember the facts and actually enjoyed listening. Their grades improved, their success increased and their retention of the material was forever stronger. Thinking back into your past, you will most likely remember a punch line to a joke, before you ever remember the formula for a trigonometry question.

Laugh though you might, the information sharing was successful because "A spoonful of sugar helps the medicine go down." As a teacher, this method has continued to invoke laughter into all the works and as a result has helped individual sharing of this knowledge with people from all walks of life.

INTRODUCTION

It seems that every aspect of our ordinary lives is being constantly bombarded by the world of high-tech. Everywhere you look there are new ways to communicate like text messaging, computer acronyms, techno-babble, and web browser developed slang used in chat rooms and on web sites. So much so, that the everyday novice could easily be overwhelmed.

Our homes are being invaded by digital transmissions of multimedia entertainment, cell phone usage, Blackberry's, and refrigerator touch screens for direct food ordering from the local supermarket. Most individuals feel the need to go back to school in order to read medical journals, or take a course in accounting in order to understand the IRS tax forms and their explanations.

We now have this new world technology where the everyday housewife needs a degree in microcomputer engineering just to download an OPRAH show. Every newscast today uses computer terminology in its reporting without realizing that the general public may or may not be up to speed with the words being used. MSNBC, MSCBS, and others just "assume" that the public is sophisticated enough to comprehend.

This light-hearted look at the terms used to translate technology verbiage into plain "English" should help the average person accept this adaption with a spoonful of whimsy. The "STANDUD GEEK DICTIONARY," has been designed to be a comprehensive and authoritative source of "Daffynitions" for the world of computer users. Some of the explanations are one way of expressing the frustration of understanding. However, the actual computer terms listed are real, only their definitions have been "edited."

WHO SHOULD USE THIS BOOK?

This book is designed to meet the needs of people who want to understand the wacky world of computer terms for use in networking, communications on the Internet, information gathering, and the general means of talking with people who, "Think Geek."

Most individuals feel slightly uncomfortable when engaged in a conversation with people who seem to have an "expert" view on things, without actually having any formal training. They have the ability to "Talk" about the subject by using correct terminology without really knowing what the words mean.

As an example, how many of us know how words were created, like the word BANK. We know it is where we put our money to be safe, but how did the word BANK get created? Who thought it up? Would it interest you to know that in the western part of the United States a few hundred years ago people lived in red adobe brick homes. They used gold dust as a means of currency and when they went to sleep at night they would hide their bag of gold dust in a little "nook" in the red brick wall to keep it safe. This Brick Adobe Nook is where the acronym BANK came from.

By having a clear understanding of what was in the mind of the person, or group of people who created these words, we can live in a comfort zone when conversing with others. For those individuals who would really like to use words that they know the meanings of, this book became a necessity.

WHAT YOU WILL FIND IN THIS BOOK

The intention of this book is to help anyone understand why an entire new method of communication has been created in order to talk to a machine that has been given the incredible distinction of "Artificial Intelligence." There are few people who can actually claim that they have any form of "natural" intelligence, much less give credit to a man-made device which can be given it "artificially."

Everyone knows that anything that has been created by man has a plentiful share of flaws, errors and downright mistakes associated with its creation. So it should not be at all surprising that all the language(s) that have been invented, all the "acronyms," abbreviations, short-hand notations and the rest would have an inherent "problem" or natural errors in them. It is with this thought in mind that what you will find in this book is a thoughtful, fanciful, and sometimes wacky view on the meanings, and sometimes hidden (Subliminal) understanding, of a world that has completely changed how mankind shares information.

The terms used are the real words created in the High-Tech world of computers. They have not been edited or in any way altered. The "Daffynitions" or, wacky definitions supplied in this book are merely a way of looking at this somewhat complex means of communicating in a more light-hearted, humorous way.

The English language is difficult enough, without adding words that are confusing to begin with. Most Americans think they speak "English", but instead have reinvented the spoken word into a sort of personal zone of their own environment, peer group, or State of residence. "I" before "E" except after "C" is no longer correct, yet everyone who was taught this in grammar school still believes it. One and one is two, accept in Binary, where it is three. Therefore the computer terminology expressed in this book may seem rather ludicrous at times, however, it is because of that fact that specific wording was created.

Only 25 years have elapsed since the inception of computer terms used by the general public. Compare this to the development of the spoken word over the past millennia and you can begin to understand why these words are in their "Infancy", or at best, were created by infantile minds during a slow growth process of understanding. The human brain is the least know organ of the human body, our thinking process is dependent on input, and without it there can be no output. Therefore having accurate input is essential for accurate output. Putting it mildly, if we cannot communicate information intelligently, why should it be expected that anyone would gain intelligence. Garbage in, garbage out, as the expression goes.

The "Stan 'Dud' Geek Dictionary" is designed to be a comprehensive and authoritative humorous look at the all-too complex definitions of the world of computer communications terminology. This dictionary includes terms drawn from a variety of topics which may include, but are not limited to;

E-Mail and Intranet communications;
Information processing of memory and memory management;
Data creation and data storage;
Internet protocols, Internet security, and the Wide World Web;
Software engineering concepts;
Programming languages;
System Operations and environments;
Hardware architecture;
Chips, Cards, and Boards;
Disks, Drives, and other Media;
Peripherals and Processors.

The order of presentation is alphabetized by letter. Spaces, hyphens, and slashes are ignored. Numbers and symbols have been omitted as having no real purpose in expression. Entries are of two main types; the full (real) definition, followed by the "Daffynition" which is completely erroneous and contain only an authors views on "would be" "could be" or, "wanna be" terms for usage.

The full definition has been substituted (or added) with a laughable one for the sole purpose of poking fun at the complexity of computer terminology. Spelling variants were purposeful and also meaningless. Acronyms are not real words, but in the world of computers, take on their own meaning, however silly of funny.

Each of these definitions has been written in clear, standard, English? Many go beyond what is considered "Standard" and can be easily looked upon as "not so standard", or in some cases, just downright, gibberish. In order to provide additional humorous detail it became necessary to "embellish" on pre-existing words in order to give them a sense of a "conceptual understanding" as to the true meaning of a word or phrase.

TABLE OF CONTENTS

CHAPTER ONE
Terminology—The logic of terms for machines to communicate with humans at a level of understanding that can cause you a terminal illness based on trying to understand the logic.

CHAPTER TWO
Acronym sentences are the art of abbreviation, in a world gone mad with too many sophisticated terms.

CHAPTER THREE
Hardware, electrical or mechanical parts that are so hard to understand that you constantly wonder where these people are, who invented them, when they malfunction and when they are in need of repair.

CHAPTER FOUR
Software—Instructions to tell the electrical and mechanical parts how to accumulate data of the logical terms that help to confuse you so much that you wonder why billions of dollars are spent to develop newer and more complicated ways to communicate by word of mouth.

CHAPTER ONE

Terminology
Numbers and Symbols

0 wait state—(See Zero wait State) Indicates the amount of patience and understanding the average computer user has for such definitions, as evidenced by the first definition of the dictionary referring you to the last letter in the alphabet to look its meaning up.

100BaseT—(wan-Hun-dred-bas-tea)—An Ethernet standard for networks using baseband signals over twisted pair cabling carrying 100 megabits per second speed. (Now, this definition assumes everyone reading it knows the meaning of the words "Ethernet", and "Baseband", and "twisted pair", and "megabits" per second" right? Wrong!!! So guess what, first go look up the meanings to these words, then come back and re-read these definitions Instead of giving you the actual meaning to begin with or confusing you by looking up the other ones first.

Example; 100 Base T means—100 million binary digits transmitted per second over a cable using eight separate copper wires which are twisted together in pairs to help eliminate interference of radio waves in the Baseband range of frequencies.

They use a radio frequency 'baseband' transmission for voice converted from electricity over the Internet airwaves identified by its "Ether", which is a term to describe the frequency in "air." (Seems like a lot of hot air to most people.)

101 key keyboard—(Oh bee won Ben can oh bee, oops wrong phonetics.) A computer keyboard with 101 Keys (Gee no kidding, 101 keys on a keyboard that has a definition of a "101" key keyboard, will wonders never cease.)

1024 X 768— (ten-twin-tee-four-by seven-an-sick-tee-ate)—A standard/ super, VGA computer display. (Here we go again with using words and descriptions that have to assume that the reader knows what they mean. Example: How can anything be "SUPER" if it is standard? Are all standard humans SUPERMEN? How can you stick in an acronym like VGA without an explanation? VGA stands for "Video graphic adapter." No explanation of the numbers, which is the actual definition. The 1024 is the number of picture illumination units (or pixels) that go across the display screen and the 768 pixels are the number of rows that go down in the display screen, if you multiple the 1024 by the 768 it gives you the total picture illumination units that make up this displays "resolution."

12-hour clock—A clock, that expresses the time, within a 12 hour range. A "half-assed statement." (So what do you do with the rest of the day?)

24-hour clock—A clock, that expresses time, within a 24 hour range. (A full day's clock, or a complete asinine statement.)

16 bit—see 8 bit, 16 bit, 32 bit, and 64 bit. (Boy! was that informative or what???) (FYI a bit is an acronym for a binary digit, represented by a "0" (zero) or a "1" (ONE) which is actually two different levels of voltage transmitted as a coded message in groups of eight digits called a byte. A binary "0" is two volts or less, while a binary "1" is over 2.5 volts up to 5 volts of direct current.) Therefore, 8 bits meant one byte of information, then two words became a 16 bit transmission and then four words are 32 bits and so on. (Take that bit in your mouth and chew it!)

400—An HTTP status code for "Bad request". (That's a nice definition, but what does HTTP mean?) Answer: Hyper text transport protocol, or in plain English, a very fast means of moving written words and instructions. (Now all you have to explain is why a number code is used instead of a simple worded explanation, the answer to that is "IDK" which is texting code for "I do not know.")

401—An HTTP status code for "Unauthorized". (Again, why use a code instead of a word? answer, IDK.)

402—Payment required

403—Forbidden

404—Not Found (So, now I begin to see the light, Example, your 400, for 401, is 403, so, 402, and if 404, then you are OOL. In plain words your "bad request" for "unauthorized" information is "forbidden" "unless payment is received," since it was "not found," you are out of luck.)

586—The average IQ needed to use a computer.

8088—The microprocessor that the original IBM PC was based on, which had 8 bits of data, moved on an 8-bit data bus. (What's a bus? Answer, it is a multiple passenger-ed vehicle, in other words multiple lines of communication in a PC, (Oh I forgot, the term PC stands for "personal computer," and not a "Piece of C**P.")

802.X—A set of communications standards defining the electrical connections of a LAN (Local Area Network) created by an organization known as the IEEE. (Industrial Electricians and Electrical Engineers)

In other words, a group of electricians got together and decided how IT professionals can or should do their jobs in computing, without "they" themselves getting trained in how those devices work!!! Real clever!!!

1394—An IEEE standard for a plug-and-play device that supports 63 nodes per bus. That's great information, now just how can you understand what that means, without a definition of what the heck a node and a bus is?? (See Node, See Bus.) (Or, try and see the intellect that went behind the definition that tells you to read more definitions.)

Words

A—The first letter of the alphabet, (No kidding?) also, the first of 26 drive "letter" specifications, as in the "A" drive or (first) floppy drive, or the "C" drive or hard disk drive. (It's also the sign given to "a thumbs up picture" of the "FONZ", which is more than I can say about these computer definitions.)

AB—(Normally pronounced "ABBEY", as in Abbey-normal)—A switching box that allows two or more computer devices to share any peripheral. It can be manual or automatic with the use of software. (Sounds pretty abnormal to me...)

ABC—Acronym for the first electronic DIGITAL computer created by John Atansoff and Clifford Berry, A-for Atansoff, B-for Berry, and C-for Computer. (Which, explains absolutely nothing about what this device does.)

ABCP—Associate Business Continuity Professional, a certification from a disaster recovery international institute (DRII) that covers basic information about disaster(s). (Boy oh Boy, I'll say, that was certainly DRY or (DRII), where do they come up with these titles?)

ABEND—Short for an abnormal end. (This is an abnormal statement to say the least!)

Abnormal Bend—(See ABEND) abnormal means, "Not normal." Bend means, "Not straight." Roughly translated, this means not a straight answer of something that is not normal, which is bent out of shape from being straight, exactly what you might expect from a computer term.

Absolute nothing—No definition needed. (Seriously, how does one define nothing, easy, don't define it, it's nothing.)

Abstract—A computer symbol that has no real meaning and must be defined before it can be understood. (Clear as mud seen through the eyes of a blind man.)

Abstract Syntax—Independent data structure of encoding. (Another way of saying an obscure hidden tax on the vices of mankind.)

Access control—The machinery by which ordinary users pull their hair out trying to understand why they cannot get the data that Identity thieves readily access.

Accelerator board—A printed circuit board that replaces the acceleration of the main processor board with a board that accelerates the speed of the processor substantially, however, the main processor is not the only device that accelerates the speed of the processor. (Gee, that really makes sense, NOT!!)

Therefore other devices affect the over—all speed which means you need to install additional devices to enhance the speed of the accelerator. (Let's see if I got this straight, you need an accelerator to enhance the accelerator, which enhances the processing of the processor by accelerating the processing speed by way of the accelerator and additional devices which will remained unmentioned.) Ha, I thought that was going to be hard to understand!!!

ACL—Access control list—A list of tools, that you have access to in order to control the items on the list. (Wait, there's more.)

Access method—The method used to access the tools that you have access to, to control the items on the list. (Wait, still more...)

Access protocols—The instructions of the methods used to access the tools that you have access to, to control the items on the list. (Still more...)

Access rights—The right to the instructions on the methods of how to access the tools that show you how to use the tools on the list. (YUP, still more, 'ad nauseum'...)(That's Latin for, "makes me sick to my stomach!")

Access token—The security pass that gives you the right to the instructions on the method(s) used to access the tools to control what is on the access list. (And, finally.)

Access time—The amount of time it takes you to go through all the above definitions before you "lose" your patience and give up trying to access anything. (This is what the original intent of this tool was developed for in the first place?)

Account—A record keeping arrangement of files. (What most programmers do to confirm if they have all their fingers and toes?)

Accounting Machine—One of the earliest automatic data processing machines. (What programmers employ the use of, to count their fingers and toes with?)

Acoustical Coupler—A Modem that includes a pair of rubber cups that fit over the mouthpiece and earpiece of a telephone receiver to prevent external noise from being picked up. (This is yet another term to confuse instead of enlighten, why not just state it in simple terms like "PUT A SOCK IN IT!!")

Acronym-Alphabetically Correct Representation of Neologically Yclept Magniloquence (Now there's a simple daffynition!!) Here's what the unusual words mean: Neologically (describing a word that has been newly created, from French 'neologisme', meaning a newly created word); Yclept (meaning 'so called', or 'going by the name of', derived from an even older English word, 'gecleopod', the past participle of 'cleopian', meaning 'call', in turn from old Germanic language); Magniloquence (meaning 'the use of grand or powerful language'—from Latin 'magnus', great, and 'loquus', speaking). (Or, simply put in easy to understand English, A word derived from the first letters of other words that defy understanding, so that you are forced to create new words that defy understanding, so that you can talk and be understood by geeks that have no understanding, so they created acronyms.)

Active Star—A centralized computer in a star topology that is active. (Otherwise known as a Hollywood actor who is presently still under contract.)

Active X—Active means working, X means it stands for an unknown, as in a mathematical or algebraic formula. (So, this definition means actively unknown, which is pretty much what all computer terminology, tells you.)

ACTOR—An Object oriented language. A Computer Trained Oriented Reaction. (A computer that makes believe it has artificial intelligence. Hmmmm, did C3PO win an academy award? AKA A Character Title Of Recognition.)

ADCMPS—Advanced digital cellular mobile phone service—Let me use my Blackberry to tweet my secretary to call my wife to ask her if I need to bring home any milk for dinner today, and have my PC server backup this message in case I forget it so that I have documented evidence that I tried to reach her to confirm this pickup. (To add insult to injury I have to pay an additional fee for that?)

Address—A mathematical, binary coded number, created to identify the location of data by it, which IS a mathematical, binary coded number used to identify information about where it is. (Simplicity is Genius, therefore, "A location in memory" should suffice as a definition. I hope I remember that.)

Address Bus—The pathway where numerous address(s) move, to carry the confused set of mathematical binary coded numbers to other locations to be interpreted into logically analyzed data that helps to confuse yet other address locations. (Get on the bus and enjoy the ride, but remember which stop to get off at!)

Advanced—Defines something as not antiquated or backward. (Kind of like these definitions, they are not antiquated or backward, but modern confusion.)

AFTO—Another F***ing training Opportunity. (As if you "Afto" attend.)

Alpha—(Latin for "doesn't work") First letter in a computer alphabet. (See beta.) (So right at the get-go they tell you from A to Z it doesn't work.)

Alt Key—One specific key on an American keyboard that is used as an alternate key should you need to have alternatives. (Aren't all keys an alternative to all others?)

Alias—(See C name)—A computer name, a user name, a client name, or any other name which is not your name. (See how simple this stuff is to understand?)

Alphanumeric—As if it weren't confusing enough to scramble letters into a confused code, now they mix LETTERS And NUMBERS together, which makes it practically impossible to understand what they are talking about. (I,C,U, dew u c me? 2,2, bad)

Analog—Refers to a device or signal which having the property of a continuous variable strength or quantity, can assume any value within a specific range. (Finally, a word that can be understood, we all know what "ASSUME" means.)

ANSI—American National Standards Institute—A "nonprofit" organization formed in 1918 for trade development. (Boy! That would sure make me "ANSI.")

Any key—Contrary to all the published words in any/all computer text books, where it states "Hit any key" there is no "ANY" key, nor is there any nitwit key or dummy key. (However, they let you escape this dilemma with the "ESC" key.)

AMPS—Advanced mobile phone service—Not antiquated phone service. (No Mabel, get off the party line before Zeke calls the Mayor, it's a high priority message from his wife. He needs to pick up a gallon of milk on his way home today!)

APTPI—Advanced Peer to Peer, Internet (networking), an abandoned routing scheme. (Which is worse, the fact that it is advanced, and abandoned, or the fact that there is actually a definition for something that is not in use?) (See Delete), (As in DELETE this definition)

Application—Refers to a complex set of programmed software instructions on how to apply the
commands to the hardware in order to complete the
task it is told to perform for the user that requested it.
(Seems like a rather lengthy explanation for "DO IT!")

Archie—A system used on the Internet to locate files
in order to transfer them to its numerous web users.
("Jug head" was probably the guy's name who thought
this definition up!)

ASCII—(Pronounced ASS-KEY)—The lettered &
numbered keys on an American made keyboard that
makes you feel like an ass for not using a pen to write a
simple letter.

ASS—Associate Security Supervisor—An
individual certification for any individual who assists
the head of security in implementing plans to assume
(We all know what that "Assume" means), that
protection is in place for all the network data. (In other
words one ass is protecting the chief ass from making
any mistakes that make an ass out of anyone.)

Asynchronous Transmission—Numerous form(s) of
transmission(s) or communication(s), that allow
simultaneous incoming and outgoing messages at the
same time. (Sort of like five female customers in a shoe
store deciding what to buy, while trying on numerous
things, and discussing it with each other at the same
time. No one else knows what they are talking about,
and it really does not matter, since they are not buying
anything anyway.)

Attribute (At-Tribute) a measurable quality of an informational code that determine(s) its properties. Now THAT is as clear as it gets. (It certainly would be if it ever makes any sense.)

Automata Theory—The study of behavioral theories, and automated devices, their processing capabilities, and limitations. (So, computer automation is a theory and not a fact? Boy that's reassuring.)

Baby Bells—A slang term used to describe A T & T companies after their divestiture in 1984. (This is the real Internet connection and its capacity.)

Back Door—A means of gaining access to information by bypassing the security measures that were created to prevent a back door entry. (Does it make any sense to create a back door and then invent a method to prevent its use? Seems like the more intelligent way, is to not find ways to lock the door, but to not have one built in the first place.

(Kind of makes you wonder why the designers built this back door in the first place, maybe THEY needed it to sneak in and make corrections of their own errors!)

Back-end—(OK, keep your mind out of the gutter) A piece of computer hardware that requests the software to determine what, if anything, it will perform. (This will help you understand what you asked it to do, because you cannot understand anything in the first place, so you kind of back into it.)

Background—(See foreground) or three ground if you want an easier explanation first. No, wait a minute that would be the first ground.

Backbone—What it takes to tell a client what you are charging them for your computer repair work. (Actually, the main computer cable that carries the communication signal to other network connected devices.)

Backup—(See Redundancy.) An alternative copy of a file or, a computer operating system. (What you do every time you read one of these daffynitions, since you have to go back into the past to the point when you were up to understanding anything.)

Backward Technology—The ability for "newer" computer systems to communicate with "older" ones. (Actually, this is the method used to move us forward into the 21st century.)

Baud—(Not to be confused with a French tart) Named after the French engineer Jean Baudot who originally measured the transmission speed of which this word defines. The "Baud rate" of a Modem, highly inaccurate, is expressed through the "CITT" or the "Comite' Consultatif International Te'le'graphique et Te'le'phonique' or the committee for consulting with international telephone and telegraph usage. (Which means absolutely nothing worthwhile to any computer user, unless you were educated in France?)

Basic—(Acronym for; Beginners All purpose, Symbolic Instruction Code.) In other words, a beginning set of simple symbols that convert ordinarily understood American words into confusing symbols that represent easy to understand instructions(don't make any bets on that) which users never actually see, or ever convert, or use to communicate by typing words on a keyboard. (Very basic, right?)

BEER—Behavior, Effect, Expectation, Results. The headings by which to assess performance of anything. Particularly, a new procedure in computer repair or networking. (Well that explains a great deal about how technicians drink in all this data.)

Beta—The second letter in a computer alphabet. Latin for, "It still doesn't work." (Wanna BET? A?)

Binary—A word meaning two components, in computer language, in means two digits. Two distinctly different things that can never be confused for one another, as in the case of "on" or "off", or hot and cold or plus and minus, ying and yang, tall and short, fat and thin, dumb and dumber, as so on and so forth...seems to me that Bipolar, means the same thing, constantly changing from one state to another. (Especially if the police are after you.)

Bistable-multivibrator—(See flip flop) (You've got to be kidding with this one...)

BIT—A binary digit combination of "1"s and "0"s that make no sense whatsoever to any user because it takes billions of them to write one sentence of text. (Binary digit) It takes one matrix of 64 separate bits to generate one alphanumeric character, and seven passes of an electron gun shooting electricity onto the inside of a phosphorus coated screen which illuminates the pattern into a visible image. (All of that, for a simple three letter word, and they think this is easy to understand??)

Board—A group of electrical circuits fused to a thin, square or rectangular shaped, surface, with connection points and solder joints. (Bored? At least this is another way of spelling it.) The largest one in most computers is named the "Mother" board, and gave birth to a newer design which was called a "Baby" board. (See circuit board) Or, if you are bored by all of this you should not bother reading it, because it is defined as "circuits on a board." (This is really Informative, to say the least.)

BOHICA—Bend Over, Here It Comes Again. This is a common phrase for all who suffer under incompetent computer network managers. (Or, the command for rebooting a computer in order to solve the problem.)

BOOSTER—Balanced, Observed, Objective, Specification, Timely, Enhanced, Repair. (Or, I gave it a shot in the arm, which still did not fix it.)

Brainfart—Term commonly referred to as a memory loss. (For computer technicians, a stinking excuse for charging overtime rates.)

BRAN—Benefits-Risks-Alternatives-Nothing. Decision making applicable, and useful for all sorts of situations. What are the benefits and risks from a particular course of action or option or default? (Now it can be understood as to why you get verbal diarrhea from too much of this.)

BUNDY—But Unfortunately Not Dead Yet. A computer term for determining replacement VS repair costs decision.

AL Bundy—A guy married to Peg Bundy who wishes the above daffynition applied to his wife.

BURP—Bogus Useless Rejected Program—Why have a term for something you never use, sounds like the same logic applied towards Politicians.

C NAME—Acronym for a canonical name, or a name that in the past, was "CANONIZED" (put in the church canon) or, another way of saying "A respected name earned like SIR, or DR. etc" In a computer, it means a name of something that needs to be respected. (As far as I am concerned they should all be burned at the stake for Heresy.)

CADET—Can't Add, Doesn't Even Try. An assessment acronym for the numerically, and motivationally challenged. (Which, is the case for most co-processors, and mostly all computer programmers.)

Captcha—(Pronounced Capture) Completely Automated Public Torture test to tell Computers and Humans Apart. You probably have captured data from the Internet without being aware of it. A "captcha" is the distorted code you copy and type into a website form. The code is unique and random and distorted so that computers (hopefully) cannot read and re-use it, which guards websites against mischievous or criminal automated attack(s). AKA, 'denial of service attack' (DoS attack). (A better understood term would be "GOTCHA"!!!)

CARL—A Microsoft acronym, for Charting, Alerting, Reporting, and Logging. (The Husband in a family, that represents control, or, Control Assigned, Relinquished and Lost.)

CASH—Computer Assisted Self-Help. An acronym for the modern age Computer-based methods, of help desk technician services. (AKA, some "person" from India who does not understand English and tells you to hit F1, or the "any key" before you pay him.)

CASS—A certified ASS. (See ASS.) (OOPS, wait a minute, just how many of those exist in the world of IT???)

CLASS—A certified local ASS. (See ASS.) (See CASS) Gee, these guys must be in a class by themselves.

CHIP—Circuit Highway In Plastic. (One of my three sons, for those of us old enough to remember.)

Command—A set of coded instructions given to a computer by the user to cause action(s) to be carried out. Commands either typed in using a keyboard, or chosen from a menu using a mouse, or "clicked on" with an icon, (or voice activated by cursing at it for doing the wrong thing.)

Compute—A calculation based on the formula that was programmed into the memory of the computers arithmetic logic unit (ALU) resulting in a numerical result. (This does not compute, unless of course, you are a true GEEK, in which case you would not need to read this extensive explanation.)

Computer—(Compute-her) A logical analyzer (ANAL-lyzer) of mathematical computations that calculates results without ever being able to think about the loss of humanity that results from its usage. (Being very ANAL helps.)

Computer Account—An object in a container, which is part of an organizational unit, that resides in a domain which is part of a tree that resides in the forest, which occupies a global catalog. (On account of you asking what it meant, try this explanation on Sesame Street.)

Computer crime—(You are not going to believe this one.) It is the illegal use of a computer by an unauthorized individual either for personal pleasure or profit. Only a vivid imagination could have stated this any easier. (It gives a whole new meaning to the term "USER-FRIENDLY".)

Computer name—An identity given to the computer box to help un-confuse the owners as to which one computer of the hundreds of billions in existence, is yours. Sometimes, named as a canonized person as in the case of a "CNAME." A canonical name associated with a person of stature. Like a Saint, or knighted as in "SIR." Imagine all that just to make sure that the box sitting on your desk is yours. (Guess who named it??)

Compiled basic—(See compiler, see basic, see syntactic, see semantic, then see a therapist and take some valium before reading more.) Any version of BASIC that is translated into code prior to the machine(s) execution by traditionally accepted language translation interpreted by the compiler. (So what is a compiler?)

Configuration—(As opposed to Pro-figuration?) The arrangement of the process by which, the individualized setup of, a computer operating system can be edited to be used as a single stand alone computer (PC) or a networked computer user(s) terminal. (In other words, W.Y.S.I.W.Y.G. pronounced "wizzywig" the acronym for "what you see is what you get.")

Connectionless—Seems rather self explanatory doesn't it? A protocol, (a what?) or set of Internet instructions for source and destination locations, called an address, so that it can send and receive data. (Connectionless, now that sounds more like the Internet I have.)

Connectoid—A Computer term which represents an icon used in a dial-up networking connection that will also execute a script for logging onto the network connection. (Is this anything like a hemorrhoid? Because it's certainly giving me a pain in my ass.)

Container—In OLE technology (See OLE, under the letter "O" for OLE, which is self explanatory) A file that contains (thus the word container) embedded objects (I bet that smarts), embedding an object with any element. (Embedding with an element, is this a violation of netiquette?)Wouldn't it have been easier to just stop at "a file that contains objects?" And let it go at that?

Control—Management of a computer. (Far too simple a definition) The processing abilities used to maintain order and continuity of multiplexed tasks and activities that must happen at the right time and in the right place, and in the right order. Thereby, creating instructions that the computer(s) memory operating system (CMOS) can understand, interpret, and execute, and thus be misunderstood and out of control. (We should have probably stayed with the simple definition.)

Control code—Used by computer programmers to instruct, interpret, explain, and in every way get the hardware devices to do what the user wants them to do. Since only programmers use this code there is no need for computer users to bother reading this definition, so "unread" this section.

Control key—When pressed in combination with another key, this key "keys" in a command to tell another key its key worded phrase to get a public key to use a private key in order to open up the lock that is "keyed" to this code key. In other words ... (I cannot think of any other words, I guess I lost key control somewhere along the way.)

Control Logic—Since the word logic means deductive reasoning based on proper interpretation of the factors, then control of that seems redundant. Thus, this definition is "an electronic circuit that uses control data." (Do with this as you wish, I am out of control.)

Conversational Interaction—(See talking) Interaction between two parties, one transmitting and one receiving. (Humans were designed with two ears and one mouth, if used proportionately we will acquire knowledge. Computers on the other hand, never will.)

Cookbook—(Try to digest this definition) A book or manual that contains information (so far, so good) that provides a step by step approach to a simple understanding of a series of multi-complex instruction sets that can only be understood after four years in college taking a computer programmers course of study. (Try a C++ grade for that.)

Cookie—What you can make out of the understanding from the cookbook.

CPU—Central Processing Unit of a computer. (A gerbil on speed, or Concentrated Poop on Uppers.)

Crash—Word used to describe what a program or system does when it fails. A minor crash, or a "bump" (Acronym for; "But User Might Protest") or a "scratch," (Acronym for "Semi Concerned About The Crap Heap") which is often used in conjunction with the acronym "POS" for piece of sh—.)

Cuseeme—("See you, see me") A video conferencing term used as the first program to give both Microsoft Windows and MAC computers the ability to communicate in real-time video. (Sounds like, Dr. Doolittle's "Pushme-pullu" creature, and just as silly. Why not just call it what it is, I.E. Video Conferencing.)

Data—(or DAY-TA, for you Star Trek fans) A Latin word derived from "Datum" or item of information. Can be used in the singular, as well as in the plural. (Or in the case of computer complexity, "Aud Nausum," which, once again means "Sick to your stomach.")

Data Fork—The universal method of separating parts of stored document(s) such as text or numerical data. A data set is a collection of related information made up of separate elements that can be treated as a unit or individual information. (Acronym FU-Fork Universal)

Default—A choice made by the computers programmed instruction set when the user does not specify any alternative action. (In other words its "DEY" fault, not yours.)

Default Directory—Where all files you need, disappear to, that exist in the hard drive until you reformat.

Delete—To remove from memory any previously input information. (This is not "DE" way to "DE" light in "DE" termining, the correct file or document to "DE" list this information from "DE" computer.)

Delete Key—A key (on the keyboard) that has the word "DEL" on it. (How is that for a simple explanation?) The fact that you use this key to delete stuff isn't mentioned in the definition, and to make sure you did not do the wrong thing, they ask you "Are you sure?"

Desktop—The visual representation of the GUI using a WYSIWYG as an onscreen work area employing Icon's, Menu's, and Graphics to simulate a person's desk (top). HUH??? What??? Could you BE more vague??? (ALA Chandler Bing!)

Desktop Publishing—The use of a computer and specialized software to combine text and graphics to create an image using various multiple-step processors involving various types of hardware equipment and software instructions in order to manufacture an original illustration with or without photo-scanning equipment and digitalizers. The finished product is then transferred to a page-maker program which is the software that most people think of as the actual publishing software, but is actually a program that allows a user to lay out text and graphics on the screen display and thereby see what the results will be. (WYSIWYG) For refining these results these programs offer a wide variety of editing capabilities and as a final step allow a printed version of this image.

(Whew!!!!!! Talk about brevity in action, as an alternative daffynition, I offer the following, SCREEN PRINT the #$@%^%$##%% thing!!)

Destructive read—The copy of the memory is destroyed by its read. (See above definition for an example)

Dibit—A set of two binary bits representing the four possible combinations of 00, 01, 10, and 11 otherwise known as the truth table. (They lied! It is what you use to set your golf ball on before hitting it with your golf club.)

Difference—What is THE Difference? I don't know, if I did, then there would be NO difference and I would not have to come up with a definition for it.

Digest—An article in a moderated newsgroup that summarizes multiple posts submitted to a moderator. (What the hell this has to do with a computer is beyond me.) (AKA-swallow, is what you are trying to do by reading these absurd daffynitions.)

Digital to analog converter (DAC)—A device that converts a digital signal to an analog signal. (Great, that's really very helpful, DUH!!! Now, would you mind explaining what the hell a digital signal is and what an analog signal is and why it has to be converted??) Digital is a binary coded electrical signal (electrons) which need to be changed into sound waves which are audible (you can hear them) otherwise you would have to be trained in how to understand Einstein's theory of unified fields, the electromagnetic spectrum, Boolean algebra, and a whole mess of other nonsense just to send a message over a telephone line, which, by the way, nobody really gives a hoot about anyway they just "Chat" Online.

DIMWIT—Don't Interrupt Me While I'm Talking. (How most computer professionals provide solutions.)

Direct access—The ability of a computer to find, and go straight to, a particular storage location in memory. (HMMMM, let's see, *one* kilobyte of information, located within one sector of a hard drive, which is part of one device that holds billions of bytes of information, that has to travel through millions of miles of semiconductor transistors, over billions of microscopic Circuit Highways In Plastic (CHIP), from input devices connected by way of a motherboard, to output devices such as a monitor screen, (oops, sorry,) GUI with WYSIWYG, and it is accessed DI-RECTLY????)

Dirty—A communications device that is hampered by excessive noise. Most often said as, "A dirty noise" (What is this? A fart??? That is the best description of a dirty noise that I can think of.)

Disk—A round flat piece of flexible plastic (Floppy) or inflexible metal (Hard drive), Compact disks(CD's) and digital video disks(DVD's) used to store informational data recorded in a coded form for use in presenting multimedia material in audio and visual and text formats. (Or that Frisbee looking "whatchamacallit" that you slide into the coffee cup holder drawer to play something.)

Diskette—The name given to a floppy disk. (Or a small female dancer in a disco.)

Diskless—Not having a disk, (Poor baby!!!)

DOS—Disk operating system, or in English, a system that operates off of a disk. (Modern term for a "Defective operating system.")

Dot—The keyboard character used to separate one sentence of information from another. (Isn't this called a "period", ok everybody, repeat after me "Microsoft," period, com. Not Microsoft DOT com.

Dot matrix—The rectangular grid where dots appear in the matrix. (Great definition, a matrix of dots, so am I seeing dots before my eyes?)

Dot matrix printer—Based on the above description, this must mean a printer that prints dots in the matrix, an equally descriptive definition.

Double dabble—A method of converting binary numbers to decimals by the process of doubling sums and adding successive bits, doubling the bit farthest from the left, adding the next bit and doubling the sum, adding the next bit and so on, until the rightmost bit has been included in the total. (Now THAT is the best comedy "BIT" yet...)

Downsizing—By 2009 definition, the economy...But seriously folks (rim shot). The practice of moving from large scale computer systems (Mainframes) to smaller sized minicomputers.

DREAM—Dedication, Responsibility, Education, Attitude, Motivation. (Close your eyes, what do you see?) That is how computer programmers envision computer technology! (Reality—the opposite of the above description!!!)

DRIB—Don't Read If Busy. (Sounds like a usual day in this author's brain.)

Dribbleware—New "pieces" of software packaged and are released one at a time, as they become available, rather than being used as a complete revision. Companies using the "Dribbleware" technique may distribute new and replacement files on diskettes or CD-ROMS, or by downloads from the Internet. (Does this author need copyright protection?? This is a genuine computer term.)

Dumb Quotes—(Sounds like an oxymoron) a quotation mark that has the same appearance as "ordinary" quotation marks. (That's REALLY dumb, because if this is true, how do you tell the real dummy from the fake dummy??)

Dummy—A placeholder, usually a character, a record, or a variable, used to reserve space until the intended item is available, regardless if it becomes available or not. (Sounds like a real dummy to me...)

Dummy instruction—(See dummy, see non-operation, see an eye doctor if you do not believe what you are reading) A non-operational instruction.

Electronic mail—(E-Mail) —A virtual collection of Online businesses that affiliate with other businesses with the intention of increasing the exposure of each business through their fellow businesses. (Talk about being redundant, an email of an email to an email? Do not confuse an email with an alpha male, or a female, or a male mail, or a female mailman, which is a total redundancy, or any other mail.) AKA the exchange of text messages and/or computer files over a communications network such as the Internet. The best definition found is; "to send an e-mail message."

ELMER FUD—Electronic license (to) Make Everyone Remember, (Who) Failed Under (That) Dummy. SEE FUD. (Sounds like any/all computer programmers.)

Encryption-Encipher-Encode-Encapsulate—(En-confuse-en-doctrinate-en-sult)—To put something into code, which frequently involves changing its form, to disguise by a special key, to prevent unauthorized access by use of a secret, complex, set of instructions, (on how to confuse, irritate and otherwise make angry, all those users who are trying to understand just what the heck you said.)

End user—The ultimate user in its finished form. As opposed to a beginning user, the end user is at the end while the beginning user is at the beginning? (What??? This definition eludes defining.)

ENIAC—An 1,800-square foot, 30-ton computer containing 17,468 vacuum tubes and 6000 manual relay switches. Developed in 1942-46 for the U.S. Army, for the purpose of doing electronic calculations. (AKA—Enormous Nothing Inside A Container)

Enter Key—The key on the keyboard that is used to enter the information into the computer's memory devices for processing. AKA, the return key. (Hint—those that enter this mysterious domain often return a second and a third time, maybe more.)

Entry—A unit of information treated as a whole. (A whole what???) A whole statement? a whole word? A whole paragraph? A whole instruction? A whole command? Kind of makes you wonder where the term "AWHOLE" came from. (The "w" is silent)

Ergonomics—The study of people, their physical characteristics and the ways they function in relation to their environment, furnishings, and machines they use. (Hmmm, computer physiologist's, Ergo, not very cost effective.)

Ergonomic Keyboard—By studying people and their physical characteristics and the way they function, a keyboard was designed. (In other words, it took a physiologist to figure out how to bend a keyboard in half so that your wrists do not tire too quickly.)

Error—A value or condition that is not consistent with the truth. (Sounds like most of the politicians we elected into office.)

Error message—A political statement that is sent Online.

Escape key—A key on a standard keyboard that allows you to escape from the command or instruction. (Another well thought out explanation.)

Exabyte—1,152,921,504,606,846,976 bytes, roughly 1 quintillion, or a billion, billion bytes, a byte, which is eight bits, which is an acronym for a Binary Digit. So multiply the above figure by eight and you get the amount of binary digits in one quintillion. (This should assure you that the understanding of computer technology is very, very simple, YEAH RIGHT! and you thought a gigabyte was complex?)

Exit—In a program, to move from the called routine back to the calling routine. Routines have various exit points, thus allowing termination based on a variety of conditions. (Reminds me of a story where a guy goes to a doctor's office and opens the front door and inside of which is two other doors, one labeled "Men" and the other labeled "Women". So he goes into the door marked "Men" and inside of it, there are two other doors, one labeled "emergency treatment" and the other labeled "routine medical", so he goes into the door for routine medical treatment, once again inside this door there are still two more doors, one labeled "Medical Insurance" and the other labeled "No insurance", he opens the door marked "no insurance" and finds himself in the alley. This is just another daffynition of "effective data processing.")

External memory—Is the Storage of data that is not inside the memory device(s) of the computer system. (Another way of saying, someone else's intelligence not accessible inside this computer. Truly artificial intelligence.)

Extranet—A spare net, oops sorry, forget that. An extension of a communications network using Wide World Web Technology, (WWW) to facilitate it, thus allowing customers and suppliers access to shared resources.

FFFF—The Hexadecimal system code for 16 times 16, times 16 times 16. (Not to be confused for any membership to a club.)

FART—Acronym for File Access, Removal, Transfer. (Now we all know what the term "brainfart" means.) SEE Brainfart

Father file—A file that is the last previously valid set of changing sets of data. The father begets the grandfather (file) and the son immediately succeeds it. The pairs, father and son, parent and child, are independent and dependant or synonymous. (What are we talking about here, GAY files? Does this mean if your computer contains "Petabytes" that you have a "Petafile" in your system?)

Feed—To digest data

Feedback—To upchuck data

Fibonacci numbers—(You're gonna love this one.) An infinite series of mathematic numbers in which each integer is the sum of the two integers that precede it, for example; 1,1,2,3,5,8,13,21,34... and so on. Fibonacci numbers are used to speed binary numbers, (BITS and BYTES) by repeatedly dividing a set of numbers into data groups in accordance with smaller sets of numbers in the sequence. (As if you are not totally confused by now, read on...) A data set of 34 items could be divided into one group of 21 and another of 13, if the item being sought is in the group of 13, the group of 21 is discarded. Then the group of 13 is divided into a group of 8 and a group of 5 then the search would continue until the item is located. Now, the ratio of two successive terms in this sequence converges on the "magic number" which seems to represent the proportion of an ideal triangle, from the curve of the nautilus shell to the proportions of playing cards, or the Parthenon in Greece. (Well, that about sums it up for me, who said that computing was complicated?) Seems pretty simple to me, all you have to do is go to the Parthenon in Greece, find this Fibonacci guy and beat him senseless with a calculator.)

File—A complete named collection of data, like glue, that binds together all instructions, words, or images that are needed to retrieve, send, delete or copy information. (Gee, and all this time I thought a file was what a receptionist used when greeting visitors.)

FILTH—Failed in (Computer) language, try Hardware. (What most computer science majors usually defer to after their mid-term grades are posted.)

Firmware—Not HARDware, not SOFTware, but someWARE in between. Example; A microchip (hardware), with instructions (software), written onto it when purchased. Thus, Firmware. (if you have difficulty finding this, perhaps it should be called WhereWARE?)

FLA—Four letter acronym. (Wait a minute, that's a three letter acronym.)

Flash memory—(Flash Gordon's brother who has Alzheimer's disease, or, I forgot where I put my wallet, sorry honey) Actually; available memory usually in a PC card that can be plugged into a PCMCIA slot. Alternative explanation, storage of information on a device that has a male (protruded end) connection, which is plugged into a female (receptacle port) connection, (watch it now, don't go getting hot.) to transfer in or out, files and folders of information to be portable or carried to another computer system, or used as a duplicate copy or backup.

Flippy Floppy—a 5.25 inch floppy disk that has data recorded on it on both sides of the media but is used in older computer systems where only recorded data is on one side. (I guess the guy that invented this Flippy-Floppy, is a Hippy Dippy, Ditzy Witzy, Willy Nilly, kind of geek.)

Flip-Flops—This needs to be broken down, FLIP= a one sided disk, Flop, see the next definition! Beach attire for walking on hot sand! (Answer—a one sided disk that contains a floating list of operational points! Cleverly worded don't you think? Or do I have to refer you to the flip side?)

Flop-Floating list Operational Points. (Now finally, that makes sense!!)

Floppy Disk—A rounded shaped piece of magnetic material that stores a floating list of operational points. (AKA the condition of your wallet after purchasing a computer.)

FLUF—File loading (of) Unnecessary Facts. (Isn't that the normal contents of all computer files?)

Foo—A string used by programmers in place of more specific information. When variables, padding, or other such syntax gaps are encountered, a programmer will type the word "FOO" to test a string input. If a second placeholder is needed, the programmer will insert "BAR" suggesting that the origin of both represents another omission. (Now we finally know where the military phrase "FUBAR" comes from.)

FORCE—Focus On Reducing Computing Everywhere. (Gives a whole new meaning to a State workforce.)

Freeware—(Wait, is that a two word phase, I'd like to know so I can get something there.) (Publicly shared software that is not sold.)

F**K—Finest Universal Cleaner Found. AKA, Failed Using Computer Knowledge. (How Motherboards end up creating Baby boards using hot male connector insertion points.)

FUD—Failed Under Dummy. (Which Dummy, remains an unknown.)

Fuzzy logic—A form of logic used by expert systems and other intelligence applications in which variables have degrees of falsehoods that can be expressed as a probability rather than a certainty. (Let's see, we coupled the words logic and intelligence with lies and guesswork, yeah, I guess that's an acceptable explanation, if you're a politician.)

GAAP—Generally Accepted Accounting Procedures. (In Computer terminology a Contradiction of terms.)

Gate—An electronic switch, that allows input signals by an operation of Boolean logic, AKA "logic Gates." Simply stated, just like the gate on your front yard fence, it allows passage THRU it when opened. (This was not named after the founder of Microsoft.)

Gateway—A device that connects networks from inside a company, to the outside world known as the Internet. "The gateway to the Internet." (What's a Gateway, about five pounds?)

Geek—A person who enjoys cerebral activities, a puzzle freak, or a computer wizard. What used to be considered a negative term has been upgraded to a positive one? Nerd, on the other hand, still has the stigma of being negative. (See, Techie, Computer Guru, nut job, wacko, or FOO-BAR.)

Gender bender (AKA gender changer)—No, this is not an operation in Sweden, it is a device for joining two connectors that are either male, or female. (Gee, maybe it is an operation in Sweden.)

Ghost—A dim secondary image that is displaced slightly from the primary image.

Ghost—A duplication in memory, of memory.

Ghost—A copy of either an operating system, or program.

Ghost—The name of a movie with Whoppi Goldberg.

Ghost—What this author will become if he continues to keep defining the word ghost over and over again.

Giga—One billion

Gigabit—One billion bits

Gigabytes—One billion bytes, (A byte is eight bits, therefore a gigabyte is eight billion zero's and one's of the binary code signal.) (Taking a byte out of Internet information.)

Glitch—A minor problem. (Like the small "o" ring that failed on the space shuttle)

Gnomon—A computer graphics term that represents a three-dimensional axis, (XYZ). (Sounds more like a Jamaican responding to a request for a loan.)

GOMER—Get Out My Emergency Router. See Router. (A Geek device used to recover from lost data.)

GOMER PILE—Location for all useless emergency routers. (AKA, hemorrhoids, antiquated term for "piles.")

Graphical User Interface—(GUI)—A type of environment that represents programs, files, and options by means of icons, shortcuts, menus, and dialog boxes on the desktop screen. Pronounced "GOOEY" due to the fact that the action by which you use a mouse to activate this tool is very sticky.

Greeking—(Yup, you read right!)—The use of nonsense words to represent the text of a document in design samples. Derived from a Latin text beginning, "lorem Ipsum Dolor Sit Amet." (At this point you are probably saying to yourself "it's GREEK to me" and you'd be correct!!!)

Grok—To understand deeply and appreciatively. The term comes from a novel entitled "Stranger in a strange land" where it is a Martian word for "to drink", and implies the kind of devoted interest that a Martian, native of a dry planet would have in water. (What this has to do with the world of computer definitions is so far "Out there" that it might as well be from the planet Mars.)

GUI—(Pronounced GOOEY) a graphical User Interface device. (What your keyboard becomes after spilling strawberry jam all over it.)

Hack—To apply creative ingenuity to a problem or a project. To alter behavior by modifying its code, rather than running the program by its selected options. (Sounds like a New York City Cab driver, running all the red lights.)

Hacker—One who hacks (Or, you're Grandfather Elmo who smokes too much.)

Handshake—A series of signals acknowledging the communication that takes place between computers and other networked devices. (What has gone missing from the world of business since the advance of computer technology. Not at all a joke.)

Hands-on—Involving the interactive work with a computer and a user. (I cannot wait for the day that we do it with hands-off!)

Hardware—Any computer device that you can touch. (Or what you try to batter to death when it malfunctions.)

HASELL—Pronounced Hassle.—Hardware and Software Electronic License Liability. (What you have to go thru every time you use this stuff.)

Head crash—(What most computer user(s) end up doing after their fifth attempt to use a computer.) Actually, a hard disk device has failed to read or write information from its platter.

Help—By depressing the "F1" key the computer has stored helpful suggestions. (You would most likely be depressed if you think that using this key helps you.)

Hertz—(Pronounced "Hurts")—A measurement of unit(s) of frequency in cycles per second. (In other words, the amount of times it hurts when you use a computer.)

Hex—abbreviation for Hexadecimal

Hexadecimal—The definition for the abbreviation "HEX." (Did we just come full circle?) If things aren't complex enough with a binary system of codes, now they have gone and doubled the complexity with a 16 bit code called Hex. AKA, one variety of a shorthand method for coding or encrypting data messages. Example; a binary 01010011 is represented by a "53" both of which no one understands, reads, uses, or in any other way does the average user care about.

Hide—(What all help desk technicians do when they get a call from an irate customer.) —To defer the display of an active window while leaving the application running.

High memory area—Memory locations in large numbers usually above 1 megabyte. (I'd like to see ANY memory that is used in a computer to be "LOW", since every modern day computer has Gigabytes and Terabytes. (By today's standards, brain damage would mean low memory capability. Come to think of it, I guess some computers are brain dead...)

HIVI—Hardware Infrastructure Virus Infection. (Commonly referred to as "Host is Village Idiot.)

HotJava—(OK, who's got the donuts?)—A web browser that is optimized to run Java applications.

Hot Plugging—(See hot swapping, hot spot, and hot Insertion.) What with all this male and female connecting going on, it's no wonder that you have hot plugging or hot swapping and especially a hot insertion. A typical hardware feature that allows equipment to be connected and disconnected, while the power remains on. (OHHHH... is THAT what it means.)

HUHA—How Humans Have Access. (Inside Information, Heads Up His Ass!)

Hung—(Ok, whoa, now we're getting into the weird areas. Who ARE these people that came up with these terms?) Hung, is past tense of hang, which means a timing problem where data is "suspended" in memory awaiting a command to "run."

IAMS—It's A Matter (of) Security. (Since its bark is worse than its bite, most people just thinks its dog food.)

ID1oT—Identity of 10 in technology. (Actually, should be the IQ of 10, in technology, AKA IDIOT!!)

IEEE—(The sound a user makes when a large file is accidently deleted!) The acronym for the Institute of Electrical and Electronic Engineers—These are the guys who set the standards for the computer industry. (Now we know why this makes a sound like screaming.)

Illegal—(A sick bird, sorry couldn't resist it.) —Not allowed. (Man was THAT a revelation of pure intellect!)

Information Highway—See Information superhighway, see information services, see information systems, see information technology. (In other words, let's see the information!!!!!!) A mathematical discipline that deals with the characteristics and transmission of information over a communications engineered system within society.

Intelligence—(This one should be a good one...) the ability of hardware to process information. A device without it is called "dumb", for example a "dumb terminal" is a computer connected to a network that has no individual memory or information loaded in it. (Sounds like most high school students in America.)

Internet—The worldwide collection of networks that communicate with one another. The genesis of the Internet was a decentralized network called ARPANET (Advanced research project agency network) of the (D.O.D.) Department of Defense. (NO wonder we have FOO and BAR, and male and female connections, and all those weird acronyms, they don't WANT you to know what they are talking about.)

IIP—Infrastructure (of) Information Processing. (Or, a stutterer who urinates.)

IKIWISI—Pronounced "ickywissy."—I'll know it when I see it. (Computer genius incarnate.) See WYSIWYG.

IKWIWWISI—I'll Know what I want, when I see it. (Another computer genius incarnate. Sounds like my Wife when she goes clothes shopping.)

Input/output—Refers to the function of storing and retrieving data. (Unintelligible stuff typed in to a computer as unrecognizable information that you cannot understand when you read it.)

Internet—Acronym for International Network. (Better known as the wide-wide-world of confusion.)

IP—(Whoa, you need to go to a bathroom for that!!) Internet protocol—See Internet—See protocol. See IP, no wait, you don't want to see me do that. (Don't you just love how definitions send you to other definitions that send you to still more definitions.)

IP Address—(I don't know about most people but IP fluids!) A 32 bit number that identifies a computer on the Internet.

IPTV—Internet Protocol Television (Internet Protocol TV). I wonder if an acronym ever had a more serious fundamental meaning than this one? Full convergence between computers and TV is fast approaching, and its effects will be wide and deep. (Some of the programming on TV makes you go IP.)

ISDN—Integrated Service Digital Network (Or, consumers pay a large fee for "IT STILL DOES NOTHING.")

ISINTOT—Intelligent Suggestion, Information Necessary To Organize Technology. (Or to most IT Professionals, "Oh S.h.i.t I Never Thought Of That.")See SHIT

Jabber—(Jab-her) A user error that causes a continuous meaningless transmission. (Sounds like the discussion held at political meetings.)

Jitter—A distortion of communications. (Again, sounds like the discussion held at political meetings.)

Jitter-jabber (See, Jabber, and Jitter)—A redundant remark of distortion, and meaningless communication. (Why keep saying it?)

Kermit—(How did Sesame Street get into this?) A file transfer developed at Columbia University. (OH, I get it; we need college graduates to develop childish data.)

Keyboard—An input device for creating data files. (Or, where you hang your Lawn Mower Keys when not in use.)

KIS—Keep it simple. (Yeah right, simple in the world of IT?, that's an oxymoron.)

Kluge—A poorly written not very carefully designed program which does not work as well as it should. (Isn't that just like sophisticated computer people, making something that does not work and defining it!!)

LAN—(See local area network)

Local Area network—(See LAN) (Annoying isn't it!!)

Local—Not remote. Not enough information? Then allow for an elaborate explanation. Anything that is within a building, a room, a cubicle, or an office, is considered "Local." Anything therefore outside a building is considered "remote." A Local area means just that, a physical area confined by the walls of the building. Therefore a city, state or country cannot be considered a "local" network. That is why the WIDE world Web is called the INTERNET Which, is a contraction of an "Internationally connected net-work," of local area networks connected to one another.

(Since you pay the same fee for making a local phone call, versus a long distance phone call, computer users Online do not notice any difference. I THINK NOT!!)

LAP—(See link access procedure) Link access means the ability to communicate. (So, what does a LAP dance mean?)

Laptop—A link access procedure desktop device used for communication on a Network. (If that is the top, what then is the bottom?)

Legacy—A computer system or application that does not conform to the standards of performance in the technical field. (Imagine that, an actual definition for something that does not perform up to the standards it was designed to perform at. Once again, a technical definition of something that is not technically correct. (Makes you wonder why we call it artificial intelligence.)

LIM—(Pronounced LEM) Replaced IBM clones and IBM compatibles with Lotus-Intel-Microsoft equip-ment. When this equipment is turned on, it is said to be a LEM-ON system. (I am sure we all know what the word "lemon" refers to when describing equipment.)

Line-of-sight—The unobstructed path, between a sending device and a receiving device. (What I do with my shotgun when dealing with bad equipment.)

Logic—As in computer logic. Hmmm, let's see, how do you define logic? I think I should change my mind, but, what is wrong with the one I have? That defies logic, or does it? Wait a minute; did we just go off into the world of illogical thinking? Therefore logic must mean to act in a logical manner. Ok, so what does logical mean?

A logical analyzer was the description of one of the first electronic calculators, and was used to "rationally" conjecture, through abstract thinking, using algorithms and sophisticated math formulas to compute what was considered "logical." (In other words, they cannot accurately define the logic upon which they base their thinking, much less reproduce "artificial intelligence," because from absolute nothing, comes absolute nothingness.)

Logic Bomb—(See logic, when this blows up in your face.) A logic bomb is actually a sabotaged attack on a computer system that has a timer to detonation. (Image a Trojan horse with a burning fuse up its IP device. Ouch!!!)

MacBinary—(Is that with or without Cheese?) A Macintosh file transfer protocol. (See protocol, see transfer, don't bother to see MAC, he can't help you.)

Mail—(See e-mail)

MECE—Pronounced MESEE. Mutually Exclusive, Comprehensively Exhaustive.(I see... No, actually, I don't see. Based on the 2nd grade expression "mesee," I guess that makes some sense.)

Mega—Millions

Megahertz—Millions of cycles of per second. (AKA—How much hurt I feel every time I fail to log on to the Internet.)

MEGO—Mechanically Engineered Graphically Organized. (To most computer graphic artists that should be a "NOGO.")

Memory—Data stored inside the computer. (Wait a minute, what did I just say?)

Memory leak—When programming information causes malfunctions due to the loss of memory. (If you have already conjured up a daffynition for this one, nothing needs to be said.) (A memory leak, is that what IP?)

Micro—Very small, as in "microscopic." (Usually the size of the programmers brains.)

Microchip—Microscopic circuit highway in plastic. A super small memory processing device. (Kind of like most computer technician(s) capacity.) (See CPU.)

Microcomputer—A really, really, small computer. (I wonder what they will use next to key in the instructions, perhaps the antennae of a fly.)

Microsoft—Microscopic software. Brand name of the largest software manufacturer. (Nerd Term for Most Intelligent Customers Realize Our Software Operates Financial Tactics)

MIME—(See multipurpose internet mail extension.) Now THAT Daffinition is not worth touching with a ten foot pole. (As if a mail extension could be that long.)

MO—Magneto-optical storage.—Capable of storing 5.25GB on a 5.25inch disk drive. (If this is MO, where are Larry and Curly?)

Modem—Contraction of modulate and demodulate, alternative words for send and receive. (What you did when the grass and weeds got taller. Watt we need is Mo of DEM.)

Modem Eliminator—Providing connectivity without a modem. (A huge hammer, or making it null and void.)

MOE—(See Microsoft office Expert) (OK, Now we have MOE but we still have not found Larry and Curly)

MOODLE—Modular Object-Oriented Dynamic Learning Environment. (Sounds like a hair-lipped Poodle.)

MOP—Measure of performance. (Or, what tool computer technicians use to clean up their mess.)

Multimedia—More than one Media.

Multimode—More than one mode.

Multiplexer—More than one Plexer.

Multivirus—More than one Virus.

Multi angry—What you should be from reading ALL THESE DUMB DAFFYNITIONS.

Multitasking—What you are asked to do with a computer in order to justify its cost.

Multiuser—(See server service) try getting two thumbs on the spacebar at the same time.

Nano—(Mork from Ork, you've been outdated.) Refers to one billionth of; I.E. a second, a technology, a unit of measurement, (or in the case of a wacked out comedian, a new language used to confuse everybody.)

NAT—Internet Acronym for "Network Address Translation." (The brother of "SID" and "SAM.") See SID and SAM.

NEET—Not Employable, Educated or Trained. (Most common Network administrator.)

Netiquette—A contraction referring to the unwritten rules of network etiquette, or how to politely communicate over emails and other network services. (Darn !!! Now I cannot tell them how I really feel when the network goes down.)

Network—A group of computers that share data through a centralized storage unit called a Server, mainframe or database. (Also may refer to the amount of work that is accomplished after all the errors are removed.)

Network Backbone—(See backbone)

NIGHTMARE—Network Infrastructure Gone High Tech Managed (by) Administrators Recently Educated. (Now there's an accurate statement!)

Node—Any connected device in a network (For our neighbors in the south, Node means something previously known.)

Null—Nil, nothing, zilch, nada, zero, none, no value, and a binary digit set to zero value. (Too much information for nothing.)

Null Modem—A modem that does nothing. (Actually it sends a signal to itself to test the circuitry, but does not actually modulate or de-modulate anything.)

Object—Any distinct entity. (Could you elaborate a little so it is actually distinct?) Any file, word processing, spreadsheet, folders, text, fax machine, printer, server, computer, user, or devices. Basically three major categories, hardware, software, and user.

Object linking—Connecting of objects. (Whoa, real rocket science definition that!)

OOPS—(Yup you guessed it! Error expression, exclamation of goof up, admission of lack of knowledge, or embarrassment of getting caught.) In reality, it means "Object Oriented Program(s)."

ORB—An object makes a request and sends it to the Object Request Broker. (In other words if you want any object you must consult your ORB. Take that! Mork!)

Open desktop—A GUI that comes from SCO that gives you FTP for ARP to use UNIX for OSI. (And you thought that learning computer terminology was going to be difficult, HA!)

Operating System—(OH MY ASS!) Pronounced phonetically "O" my "S") the software instructions or program that "tells" the hardware how to work the system of the computer.

OSI—Open Systems Interconnect, used as a "layering" method of moving data On the Internet. (OH, I SEE...)

OS2—Operating system mouse device version 2. (Better known as Obsolete soon too!)

OSPF—Open the shortest path first. An internet instruction for getting the data transmitted the quickest possible way. (The acronym should be reality based as "TILMD" for "The Idiot lost My Data.")

Packet—Any sized group of data sent over a network. (Sort of like that Christmas package you said you mailed by parcel post six months ago without putting a return address label on it.)

PAD—Packet assembler and dis-assembler. A network device, that converts a serial data stream from a bridge, into a "fluid" moving message transmission and back. (Seems that raising the river instead of lowering the bridge, is an effective methodology. Or, perhaps they are "Padding" it too much.)

PANIC—Acronym for, "Program Access Networked Infrastructure Computing." (For most network Administrators it means "Pressured, And Not In Control.")

Password—(Stop! Who goes there? Oops, sorry, wrong movie.) A security method of identification used on a computer network system that almost never actually does anything accept force you to write down the outrageously long darn word you can never seem to remember.

PB—Peta byte, Peta for quadrillion, and Byte for eight bits. (In other words, the length of texting your daughter at college has billed you for, this past week.)

Pentium—Type of Central Processing Unit (See CPU), trade name. (Acronym for Profoundly enormous numbers that incorrectly understand math.)

Petafile—(Don't go there!) A file that has quadrillion bytes of data in it. (Actually a fictitious term designed for this book.)

PC—Personal Computer. (Why they are called a "Personal" computer is a misnomer, since every hacker can invade it.)

PCMCIA—Personal Computer Memory Card Industry Association. (The best daffynition for this is "People Can't Memorize Computer Industry Acronyms.")

Peer to Peer network—A network where users can communicate with each other directly, without the need for intermediate devices. (If you believe that it is because it a"PEERS" to be doing that.)

Period—The "." Character, on every keyboard that is used to separate the first part of a computer file name, from the last three digit(s) part. (I.E. Microsoft.COM, spoken Microsoft "DOT" com, instead of what it really is, which would be spoken Microsoft "Period" com.)

PDA—Personal digital assistant. (Boy, would I like to give you a personal digit, guess which one!) A tiny computer which, you use with a pen or stylus, to e-mail or otherwise connect to database information.

PICNIC—Programs In Computers, Networks, Infrastructures, and Clients. (Most times it means "Problems In Confusion, Not In the Computer.")

PING—Packet internet grouper command of TCP/IP used with ICMP to communicate with your ORB to see if your ARP is in connection to your MAC so that you can use your PC with OSPF to have OSI give you HTTP within a specific TTL. (Whew...now that's a lot of CCRRAAPP, no acronym intended.)

Ping of death—A very special ICMP message designed to crash the computer it is sent to. (And all this time I thought it was a lottery winning notification!)

Plug and Play—A device that is recognized by the computer's program instructions and can automatically "play" this device without any editing being done to the operating system by adding software to the computer's memory. (What most users do when things do not work automatically and their boss is not watching them log onto the Internet to the "Game" page.)

POP—Point of presence, or Post Office Protocol—A connection to a telephone company that transmits e-mail messages. (They cannot seem to make up their mind as to what acronym they want to use, so they have two meaning to the same one. Who said computer terminology was complex?)

Port—The connection point for most external devices to a computer. (I do not know about you, but this is what I reach for a glass of, when I am forced to memorize these acronyms.)

Port Number—65,535 available numbers for the default identifier for transmission over the Internet. (Now you see why pouring a glass of port is necessary.)

Portable computer—As if a definition were necessary, it is a type of computer small enough to be carried easily, like a Laptop or Notebook. (Try doing this to the ENIAC.)

POST—Power on self test, a set of diagnostic routines that the computer performs before starting its operating system. (The computer is at its post, doing its thing before it lets you pass by into its inner workings, kind of like a guard at the door that checks you before allowing you to come in to work.)

PPP—(Not what an infant or octogenarian does when they lose control.) Acronym for a "Point to Point Protocol," refers to the instructions for direct contact over the internet, like a person-to-person phone call.

PPPP—Programmable Peripheral Printer Port. (Better yet, "Piss Poor Project Planner.")

PPTP—(Not when an infant or octogenarian loses control in an Indian's teepee.) It is the protocol that "tunnels" under the traffic and avoids collisions.

Pretty good privacy—(Is this where all that hot insertion, hot swapping male and female connections take place?) A popular public key encryption. (I cannot understand how something public can be private, do you?)

Primary—The first, the premier, the beginning. (Unless we are talking about a Presidential primary, then its kill or be killed, first!)

Primary domain—The first group of logically arranged computers. (Logic? Who's Logic.)

Primary domain controller—The device that is in control of the first logically arranged computers. (Now all we have to find out is, who is in control of the controlling device.)

Printer—A device used to create a hard copy of stored data or files. (Or, a joke in poor taste consisting of a jammed paper trail, leaking ink, and burnt paper.)

Private key—The secret portion of the public key encryption shared by the public key holder. (Let's see now, a private key shared by a public key holder, hmmm...sounds like you just give the executive washroom key to a homeless wino.)

Programmer—A person who writes code to instruct the computer hardware in the task it is to perform. (Or, high school nerds with white tape on black glasses who played Dungeons and Dragons, memorize Star Trek episodes, who are now millionaires who create "user friendly" software to get revenge on students in high school who gave them noogies.)

Promiscuous mode—A mode which uses ALL the packets it can capture in its web, not just those addressed to it specifically. (OH... this is where all that male and female connections of hot insertions and hot swappable take place. Great name for it.)

Propagation—(The result of all that promiscuous mode, hot swapping, hot insertion connections.) —In communications, the delay between the time a signal is sent and received.

PU—Yeah, it stinks, but we have to give it a daffynition. Acronym for a "Physical unit."

PURE—Product Use Replacement Electronics. ("Previously undiscovered Repair Error.")

PURE CRAP—"Product Use Replacement Electronic Computer Repair and Programming." (Now, an obvious definition. (see above.)

Quality of service—This defies definition, especially if you have a home in the remote part of town.

Query—(Not a person living in San Francisco)—Extracting and displaying data, specific data.

Queue—Pronounced "Q"—a list of items waiting to be executed. Example, in a printer, a list of print jobs waiting their turn to get their job done. (Not to be confused with the guy who supplied James Bond with all his gadgets.)

RAD—Rapid application development. (What most young computer "gamers" think of the new DVD they just bought.)

Radius—The acronym used to describe the "Remote Authentication Dial in User Service". (As long as the radius is not more than a few feet, and you are using someone else's WAP.)

RAID—(A device used to get rid of the bugs in your computer?) Acronym for a Redundant Array of Independent Disks, another way of saying it takes more than one brain to compute data.

RAM—(What you do to install a hot insertion device using both male and female connections?) but seriously folks, RAM is random access memory, which is basically the same as trying to find a needle in a haystack with boxing gloves on, while suffering from dementia.

Read-only—About all you can do with most computers today without getting into trouble.

ROM—Read-only memory. Permanent information stored in a computer even when the power is turned off. (See flash memory.) If I could see memory in a flash, I wouldn't need permanent memory and what about permanently LOST memory? How do you get that?

Real mode—As opposed to fake mode???—Directly accessing the first 1 megabyte of memory, which, to say the least, does not allow for very much to be done. (So, does that mean that all other memories above 1 megabyte are "UNREAL" mode?)

Reboot—The term that means to restart the computer after it has failed for one reason or another. (A very appropriate term due to the fact that most people want to kick the computer a second or third time for its failure.)

Registry—A system database that contains configuration information. (The front desk of the hotel, or motel, where that entire promiscuous mode with hot insertion, hot swapping male and female connections take place. I'm beginning to see where the mind's of computer hardware inventors is located.)

Remote—Not local. (Great definition.)

Remote connection—Not a local connection. (Another great definition.)

Remote desktop—(Yup, you guessed it,) Not a local desktop.

Remote user—(OK, I give up, what does remote mean?) Not a local user.

Repeater—What a hardware device does to any local data. (What the last four definitions did, they kept saying the same thing over and over without ever telling you what it means.)

Return key—What you press when you are feed up with this lousy computer.

RISK—Reasonable Identity System Knowledge. (What happens when you take the word of a systems technician.)

Root Directory—A directory of directories, which cannot be deleted. (In other words, once the harm has been done you cannot undo it.)

ROSA—A Microsoft acronym for, "Request Offer Select and Accept," a lease of network address for computer workstations and servers. (Also, Carl's wife, who has control.) (SEE CARL.)

Router—An intelligent device that determines the pathway that all data will flow along. (Wait a minute, did they say intelligent? How did that word get into computer technology?)

RIP—Router information protocol—The instructions on how to route data over a network. (Yup, that makes sense, every time they transmit information over the internet they RIP you a new one.)

SAM—Security accounts management—The file that contains the information regarding the correct identity of network users. (Putting it another way, the guy you blame when you have no security on the Internet.)

SAN—Storage area network.—Where information is put to secure it from getting lost. (There are storage area networks contemplated for the Moon, only problem; who is going to fix them when they need servicing?)

Sandbox—(Where most of the computer programmers got their intelligence from.) Actually it refers to Java programming systems where the Java applet may execute, but it cannot read or write outside the sandbox. I think this is where the expression "Thinking outside the box" came from.

SAP—Service advertising protocol, or what most people feel like after they paid for their computer and THEN hooked it up.

SATAN—Security Administration Tool for Analyzing Networks. (Remember, the words in this book are the actual computer terms, only the daffynitions have been edited.) So this now explains a great deal, we have Satan as the administrator of network analysis. This is anything BUT funny.

Schema—A term used to describe objects and properties and how they are used in a database. (This term no longer surprises me, now that the previous definition has been disclosed.)

Scripting—The process of writing script for the computer to follow. (Now that makes sense, I always knew computers were acting funny, now I know who gave them their lines to follow, a bunch of comedians who play in a sandbox.)

SCSI—(See SCSI terminator) (Or, what you think of when you change your three month old underwear.)

SCSI Terminator—(No, it's not Arnold.) SCSI is the acronym for a small computer system interface, and terminator means where the message terminates.

Secure MIME—(Not secure yours, but secure MIME.) MIME—Multipurpose mail extension, which is secured. (I can see why it is important to secure your mail extension, what with all that hot insertion and hot swapping going on with male and female connections in promiscuous mode.)

Security—Operating system tools designed to prevent unauthorized access to data files. (What most computer users are willing to pay a great deal for, but have yet to get their monies worth?)

Serial—A single transmission of data. (Sending one bit at a time.)

Serial Rapist—(Not a computer term, but one way to get back at "Captain Crunch.")

Server—Any computer that provides service to its users or clients for accessing of files, Internet connectivity, and sharing of hardware devices. (Amazing, actually serving someone with something, without giving them a tip.)

Share—Refers to a device, an element of software, or another user's information, commonly referred to as "Hardware-Software-User." (Also known as, Moe, Larry, and Curly.)

S.H.I.T—Server Hypertext Information Transport (The definition kind of says it all.)

Short—(See short Circuit.) No thanks; I am not interested in lame robots that keep crying for "More input" More Input.

Short Circuit—When two wires cross each other and cause the flow of electricity to take a shorter route back to where it came from without ever completing its path. In a computer this means the entire instruction never got through, or that part of the instruction got through only a portion of the way thus making the entire message incorrect. (Whew, why not just call it what it is, See "FUBAR".)

SID—Security Identifier (The brother of SAM.) See SAM

Signature—A "short" text file that is automatically added to the end of your e-mail or other sent data which usually contains your name (or alias) which may contain some pithy quotes; whatever your signature file contains, remember to keep it "short". (Just like this definition.)

SLED—Single Large Expensive Disk—As opposed to RAID, which at one time in the past was known as Redundant Array of Inexpensive Disks. (So to be computer literate you must not have "SATAN" "RAID" your "SLED", you would be a "SAP" working out of the "SANDBOX," this would be a "FUBAR," and you would be taking "SAM" out of the "SAN" and "RIP" "PING" him a new one.)

Sneaker net—A method of sharing data by copying it onto a floppy disk drive and carrying it to another computer. (Boy, what an Idiot I am, I've been using sneaker net all my life and did not know how sophisticated I was.)

SNIFFER Sniff Electronic Records—A network analyzer tool, which "Sniffs" the equipment for problems and communicates with the user as to what it discovered. (Kind of like a hound dog, except when it is sniffing other dogs, like "RIPPING" them a new one.)

Socks—A protocol of a secure SOCKET, used to control internetworked communications. (Oh, now I understand, we use a sniffer to check out our SOCKS.)

SOHO—Small office, Home office. (Not if you are in San Francisco.)

SOM—System Object Model. (Som definition.)

SPA—Software Publishers Association. (So, you use a SPA to get a SOHO pair of SOCKS and sniff them to see if they have any problems.)

Spoofing—A make believe user, who is breaking the secure nature of the network to gain information. (Sounds like all students studying to be computer scientists.)

SWAN—A secure wide area network. (And all this time I thought it was a white duck.)

Syntax Error—When computer wording is incorrect. (To the everyday consumer, it is when you walk into a computer store and say "Money is no object.")

Task—Work that is performed on a computer. (You Hope!)

Task manager—The programmed written instructions, that tells the computerized device what to do. (Loose definition—Wife!!)

TTL—Time To live—A method incorporated into network transmissions to prevent data from continuously traveling along the wiring forever. (This definition should apply to the repairmen who never seem to fix the problem within the hourly rate they charge you.)

Time Synchronization—A method of synchronizing time on a network. (Is this a definition or an oxymoron? How can you have "Time" without synchronizing it? Furthermore, how can you synchronize anything without timing it?)

TOP—Technical Office Protocol—(See MAP—Manufacturing Administration Protocol.) Once again definitions that direct you to other definitions, but fail to define the word you needed to know the definition of in the first place.

Transmission Control Protocol (TCP)—Transmission control instructions of how to transmit and receive data correctly over a wired network without error. (Without error? Sounds like "Houston, we have a problem.")

Tree—(Not two but Tree.) In a network arrangement, a tree contains many branches that split off from the trunk. (Typical computer logic, unless your "barking up the wrong tree.")

UART—(Pronounced You-Art) A Universal asynchronous receiver transmitter. (Yeah, when they work right, otherwise they are called you-art wrong.)

Undelete—Is that anything like UN-pregnant? How do you UN-erase something? In computer terms it means to recover from an accident. Isn't that the meaning of the word "Heal"?

Unicast—An individual broadcast of information. (The name of the device that is put on the broken leg of one computer technician, after he presents you with his bill for services.)

UPS—(Pronounced you-pee-ess) (I do not know about most people but Eye - Pee - Pee) Means "Uninterruptible Power Supply" or, a battery that kicks in when power is lost, so that data is maintained without failure.

USER—Uneducated scary electronic retard. (Yup, we are addicted!)—Any person allowed access to a computer system or a network. (And the only cure is use-less, or makes it useless.)

    1."Novice User"—People who are afraid that they will destroy everything by touching it.

    2."Intermediate user"—People who know that they will break it by touching it.

    3."Expert user"—People who know how to fix what they break by touching it.

User friendly—Pertaining to a device or, software that only the Programmers understand how to use.

UUCP—(Pronounced you-you-see-pee.) (Sounds like you saw a ghost urinate.) A Unix Utility used to transmit to newsgroups.

UUDECODE—(Pronounced you-you-de-code.) (Talk about redundancy, this is bad enough without having to say it twice.) A Unix Utility that converts a signal back to Binary. (You, you, better, better, get, get, this, this, correct, correct.)

Value added process (VAP)—An application that adds value to the function. (Do we take that to mean that without VAP it is a valueless function? Seems a little strange to create something that is valueless and then add something to it to make it of value. Or, is this the way programmers cover up their mistakes?)

Vampire tap—A connecting device that uses two needle points to penetrate the insulation of a wire to make a connection to the wire within. (How they suck your wallet dry by overcharging you for service you do not receive, and the only way you know it, is by the two holes in your pants pocket.)

Vertical Bar—A symbol on a keyboard "|" used as a wall to separate sentences. (Where you go to get a vertical drink after reading all these vertical daffynitions, written by some computer geek, who is never found in a vertical position.)

Virtual—Real, but not really real, instead, make believe it's really real, even though it isn't. (This requires explanation!) A Virtual connection makes believe it is actually connected, when in fact it was connected once, but continues to act connected, even after it has been disconnected. So, George Washington is a Virtual President. (What this actually means to computer terminology is beyond my understanding, you either have it or you do not, it's either real or unreal.)

VPN—Virtual Private Network—A Private network that is not really private but acts as if it is private. (No wonder my identity is being stolen!!!!)

Virus—What I am getting from reading all this diseased information, which is why I have to go to a vertical bar and have that drink while I am still vertical. An actual computer virus is a program that is intended to damage the computer system without the user's knowledge of it. (Well, that explains what my wife has been doing to the computer behind my back, only she uses a hammer.)

WWW—Acronym for the Wide World Web. (To most users, is stands for the wide world of waiting.)

Wait State—What all users do when they pay as little as possible for Internet connectivity. (AKA the U.S. Armed Forces chow hall)

Weak Password—Any password that is easy to guess, like any reference to Star wars, or Star trek. (This is a real definition!) (Who in the world would think that humancyborgcp3o is an easy name??)

Windows—A Microsoft name of a type of Operating system. (To IT professionals it is something the "Will Install Needless Data On the Whole System.")

WORM—Write Once Read Many—Also known as a write-back, which means it can be written once but read many times. (Apparently, programmers need to re-read what they write many times, before it makes any sense to them, now that clears up the confusion real good.)

Z—The last letter of the American alphabet.

Zero Administration Kit—Self explanatory, do nothing.

Zombie—A dead process that has not been deleted that may appear from time to time. (How can a process which is dead, be deleted, or not deleted, and why would it appear from time to time if it is indeed a dead process? This can easily be misinterpreted as Horror!)

CHAPTER TWO

An example of acronym Sentences

CARL and ROSA need SID, SAM, NAT, and ARP to have a WIN.

Translation—Charting, alerting, reporting and logging, needs a request, and offer, and a selection, plus an acknowledgement from the Security ID# account and the security accounts manager in order to have a network address translation to get an address resolution protocol to have a Windows internet naming service provide connectivity. (I guess speaking geek has its advantages after all.)

R, U, getting ANSI because you AFTO, BOHICA and KIS my ASS.

Translation—Are you getting the American national standards institute because you need another F**king training opportunity, well bend over, here it comes again, so keep it simple my Associate Security Specialist.

PC OSPF OSI HTTP TTL NIGHTMARE

Translation—A Personal Computer needs to open the shortest path first in any Open systems interconnection using hypertext transport protocols before the time to live expires and the network infrastructure which has gone high tech manages the administration which was recently educated.

SPA SOHO SOCKS SNIFFER

Translation—Software Publishers association thru a small office home office needs to secure a socket in order to sniff electronic records.

SATAN PURECRAP

Translation—Security administration tool for ana-lyzing networks products usage, replacement, elec-tronic, computer repair and programs.

NEET PC USER

Translation—Not employable, educated or trained personal computer user.

DIMWIT BEER BURP BRAN BUNDY, SCRATCH ASS.

Translation—Don't interrupt me while I'm talking my behavioral effect, expectation, results are bogus, useless, rejected programs due to benefits, risks, alternatives, or nothing, but unfortunately not dead yet. So, being semi-concerned about the "crap" heap with your associate security supervisor won't help.

DRIB FART IAMS NEET HUHA FILTH

Translation—Don't read if busy this file access removal transfer because it's a matter of security when the technician is not employable, educated or trained, and heads up his ass is a definition because he failed in language so he tried "hardware."

WORM TOP USER TTL SATAN

Translation—Write once read many times the technical office protocols of an uneducated scary electronic retard so that they have time to live before the security administration tool for analyzing networks gets them.

CHAPTER THREE

Hardware

Hardware is defined as anything that you can touch, therefore any part, component, device, or piece of electronic circuitry that can be handled is considered hardware. The list of hardware devices are numerous to be sure, to try and memorize all of them is unnecessary. Suffice it to say that just remembering their category should be enough to test our brain cells. The cost of manufacturing these hardware devices in the beginning of the computer revolution was slightly expensive. For example, the main circuit board known as the motherboard cost around $400.00. Today, most of them are priced at about $80.00. The repair and maintenance of these used to cost $65.00 an hour in labor, and the skills of soldering and diagnostic testing equipment made it all the more costly. Today, they are simply swapped out with new boards, and therefore the job of hardware repair became easier and more cost effective. Like most computer repair technicians of the past, their technical knowledge and hands-on skills took a great deal of learning and practice. The more modern computer technician merely needs to know how to remove and replace the defective component, without having any real in depth knowledge of how or why it works. As a result of these "modular" devices, the training costs were diminished, and the ability for some "non-technicians" were increased. Most people today will change some computer parts, but when the computer malfunctions to where the everyday user does not have the know-how to fix it, they still rely on a skilled computer technician to solve these problems. Hardware problems have been minimized by the "solid-state" method of manufacturing these parts, and by making them at a vastly reduced cost, has almost eliminated their need to be repaired. The fact that newer, more efficient, and smaller computer equipment is constantly being improved upon, by the time some part does break down it's time to buy a newer model anyway. Since almost all "PC's" are now a part of a network of connected computers, the devices known as hardware are "Network" connectivity equipment such as Routers, Gateways, Switches, and most important of all, Servers. Software is at the heart of the matter and becomes the most profound understanding, and in most cases is responsible for almost all computer problems. Therefore the study of the instructions that tell the hardware devices what to do is of critical importance. The following list will outline the various hardware devices and their usage.

List of Hardware Components
Internal parts—Think inside the box
External parts—Think outside the box, AKA Peripherals.
Wire connections—Cables, connectors, extensions cords.
Distribution Devices—Hubs, Switches, Routers, and Gateways.
Servers—AKA Mainframes or centralized databases.
Workstations—Networked computer user(s) equip ment

So, following the old adage that simplicity is genius, the categories of hardware are; internal parts called "chassis components" this phrase means the box that houses the various devices that make the computer "compute." The internal parts are very simple, there are a total of seven, *three drives, three circuit boards, and one power supply.*

The "drives" are called; the hard drive, (Because it is made of aluminum and is hard to bend), the CD-Rom Drive (Because it is compacted data on a small disk.), or a DVD drive, (Because it contains digital video, and audio, information on a disk.) and the floppy disk (because is so flimsy that it flops and flops like an overcooked piece of spaghetti, And the more up to date, larger capacity storage device known as a USB drive. (Because it is universally transmitted over a serial (one lane) bus, multiple passenger, carrier.

You can always install more than the three that come as standards, but that would make things more complicated. (Far be it for any computer manufacturer to make it complicated.)

Then there are the three circuit boards, another way of saying this is the electronic wiring that moves the data in electronic coded signals from part to part and from inside the box to the outside of the box. (The "BOX" is a nerds term for the chassis.)

The three circuit boards are the main system board referred to as the "Motherboard", and the two cards it gave birth to, known as the Video board (or card, as it is commonly called) and the I/O card which is a standard name for a circuit that can be used for a number of different functions which communicate in (I) and out (O) of the box. Hence, an Input/output or I/O circuit board.

Finally the power supply receives 110 volts of alternating current, (AC) from a wall outlet and converts it into a useable 5 and 12 volts of direct current (DC).

Next are the external components sometimes referred to as "Peripherals" or surrounding parts, called the standard input and output devices named Keyboard and Mouse, or Monitor and Printer. These comprise the standard PC system components.

Networking computer components are somewhat more involved, but can still be remembered as categories of communication devices. Network devices are categorized as follows; cables or wiring, pathway connectivity devices, and connectors.

The cabling comes in three types; the first and cheapest is a twisted pair type that comes in shielded and unshielded varieties, of 7 categories. The second is coaxial cables that are named "Thicknet" and "Thinnet" and mean just what they say, one is thin and the other is thick. The third and perhaps the most expensive type is Fiber Optic, which is a cable containing hundreds of minute fibers along which numerous messages flow.

Pathway connectivity distribution devices come with many names, all of which provide the same function, they "redirect" the pathway by different means, and these different means are spelled out in the names of the devices. One is a HUB, which is a centrally located distribution point, just like the hub of a wheel. The next is a bridge, which connects two different wiring connectors like a twisted pair to a fiber optic. Then there is a router, which does exactly what its title implies, and then a switch, which switches the pathway by predetermined routes. Finally the "Gateway," is a multiple translator of computer languages.

The connectors are used with each of the three varieties of cables, for twisted pair there is an RJ-11, for telephone wiring, and an RJ-45 for computer cabling. (RJ is the acronym for "Radio Jack.") The "T" connector or BNC is used for coaxial cabling, (BNC is an acronym for "Bayonet Nut Connector") and then the

SC and ST types are used for Fiber Optic. (SC is for "stick and click" or ST, for "Stick and Twist").

In addition to all these "connectivity devices" are the "Mainframes." This is the name given to the computer equipment that provides all the data to all the users. This equipment is known as the "Server" or, a computer which serves the client and provides it with its requests for information.

On the Internet, we have numerous "Internet Service Providers" or ISP's whose sole responsibility is to provide all its clients with the accessibility to this information.

Servers come in a large variety and have titles such as "Primary" domain controller, backup domain controller, Proxy server, Application server, Data Base Server, and more specific titles having to do with individualized programming and job functionality.

Together, all this hardware must be maintain, repaired, and most important of all, upgraded to accommodate the fast paced movement in the world of media communications. Without growing in size, and speed, it would fail to keep up with the flood of ever-increasing information sharing across the globe. For most people, the use of a computer is a complicated task.

Its purpose is ever-changing as well as the task(s) that it is asked to perform both in the business world and by individuals. Windows operating systems have come a long way in a short period of time and as a result, a constant upgrading of knowledge and re-training is in order.

Numerous books are being published, most of which are for the technician or the student. For the everyday user, navigating within any large system requires some understanding as to its structure and scope. Active Directory means exactly what its title implies. Rather than having a complex chain or string of main directories, sub-directories, and sub-sub-directories, with folders and sub-folders, and files, Active Directory works much like that of an alphabetical listing in a card catalog of a library.

To locate a resource such as a user, a printer, a shared folder, a web browser, or any utilities or tools, you simply need to look them up like you would any other database. Once you open up the Active Directory screen, you simply scroll to what you wish to access and click on it. It either takes you directly to the chosen destination or, it guides you to another directive. Regardless of how it does it, the procedure or complex string of activity of the user is simplified.

In order to have this feature activated it is necessary to load it into the computer. It needs to be coordinated with many other components of the system in order to take full advantage of its wide-ranging abilities. Most Networked computers have some sort of a backup system.

For the everyday user this is not common knowledge, however, for an administrator it is an absolute necessity. There are a number of ways in which to backup data.

The type of data to be backed up may determine the method by which it is done. For example, if you back up a file consisting of one particular document or more, it would be useful to use a floppy disk or a thumb drive.

When backing up your system files, this can be done with a set of "boot disks", when you are backing up an entire network of traffic you will need a dedicated Server that synchronizes the data minute by minute.

To have an internal backup system, you may select repeating the data on one or more disk drives; this is known as RAID, or redundant array of independent disks. Its purpose is to have an uninterrupted recovery when the original data is lost.

When choosing a level of RAID, it is best to decide which you are going to employ as they all have slightly different rules to follow for backing up data. To put it simply, they each offer a method of securing data, and they will be very helpful in recovering from a problem.

However, as is with anything, cost and efficiency is what needs to be considered first. While one method may be cost effective, it may not do 100% of what you need. Another choice may perform the exact task you wish, but may have a price tag bigger than you planned on. When you initially load an operating system into any computer, one of the steps it will prompt you to do is to create backup disks.

This step, while being important, should alert the everyday user or administrator, to consider making a few extra copies and having them secured in more than one location. In addition it is advisable to have this information put onto an "ERD", or emergency repair disk, pertinent to that specific computer.

When a computer fails to boot up, or perhaps boots up into "Safe Mode", these disks can be used to assist the technician to solve an otherwise difficult troubleshooting headache.

By the standards of today, most computer equipment is either backed up by this method, or in the case of a networked computer, it also has copies on the centralized server. This method by far is the easiest and least difficult way of recovering from a problem.

In Windows workstation(s), there is a program called "Recovery Console", this is essentially the troubleshooter helper. It has a set of files with information on them that will help recover from a software related problem, be it a stand-alone or a networked computer.

K

The process of creating back up disks is just one example of the type of instructions required and the way to make copies is a simple process. The phrase "Booting Up" comes from the old days of English Lords who had stable boys help them with their riding boots. When they abolished slavery, they were forced to put on their own boots, and the expression "Pulling oneself up by one owns bootstraps" caught on.

Today having a computer turn itself on is known as "Boot up", which essentially means that it goes through the necessary sequences to "turn itself on". The software that contains the boot up instructions is an "Initialization" file, or a file that starts this process.

The Boot.ini as it is called is used to begin the boot up process and can be modified when changes in the operating system occur. This information is also necessary on any boot disk, backup disk or recovery disk. When you load an operating system for the very first time it will ask you if you wish to make a backup disk. Here too, you will have a copy of this file, and a few others as well. Any additions, corrections, or editing that needs to be done is usually done manually when you have a Windows operating system.

In other operating systems the boot file is updated automatically, however, you still need to manually change the emergency repair disks and any backup disks you may have previously created. One of the initial Administrative tasks performed is that of setting up an account for individuals. This is classified as a "User", or a person who is a member of a network, and as such has accessibility to its numerous resources.

A User can also be a group of people in one department of a small local business, or a group of groups in a large geographical location. Some "Accounts" are automatically created when the operating system is loaded. These are known as "default" accounts. Along with having an account you also have certain "rights" or permissions to use resources within the network. These are known as "Policy", or "Trusts".

The network administrator must determine which accounts will have full permission, limited rights, or no accessibility at all, before setting up any new user accounts. They can of course be altered, merged, edited, and deleted by the network administrator as the need arises. These account setups have specific rules, such as how to name the user, and how to join a group or a domain.

The users become "Objects" and the objects become a larger grouping and so on, until they become a "forest."

CHAPTER FOUR

Software

The definition of the word software in computing is recognized as the "programming" of the computer's hardware. More specifically a piece of hardware cannot actually "DO" anything without a set of electronically coded instructions transmitted to it, with complete detailed "programs" which dictate its action or task. When you tell a newborn baby to sit up and read a newspaper, it has no understanding of your words, much less the meaning behind them, and therefore cannot comprehend anything and will simply lie in the crib and do nothing. In order for a computer and its hardware components to "do" the tasks given it, it must contain the programming instructions to carry out these tasks.

In the beginning of the world of computing tasks, there were few tasks demanded of computers other than mathematical equations and later, processing of words. Today, the modern computer is asked to perform a wide variety of functions and tasks at a greater than ever before imagined rate of speed, accuracy, and quantity. The understanding of just how these instruction sets carry out these incredible demands is by far the most complex understanding in this world of technology.

To begin to grasp the intensity of this subject, let us first imagine how a human being, using the English language, is communicating with a piece of metal using a form of energy called electricity. That statement by itself requires a hefty understanding of the bizarre. To break this sentence down into its respective parts, let us begin with human communication. Mankind has developed a means of communicating by trial and error beginning with body language, gestures, sounds, and physical aggression. Later, the use of images like pictures of birds and animals were used to represent meanings or thoughts.

Still later as mankind evolved, the use of speech was developed and has been edited, modified, and added to, for centuries. Modern mankind uses not only "structured" languages, but incorporates slang, inflections, varied pronunciation, and interleaving of foreign words into a multitude of diverse means of communications. The understanding and use of the spoken word can be poetic and entertaining, informative and constructive, mind boggling or soothing, healthy and depressing, or enlightening and educational. Its misuse can be devastating and downright annoying. A computer has no emotional capabilities.

Therefore it needs exact and specific words in order to function. Incorrect "Syntax" as it is called is reacted to as "I cannot comply with your instruction" and does nothing until it is given instructions that are in its memory chip(s).

A computer has its wide variety of languages that it uses in order to communicate with its variable parts, and it is based on codes that have been created by a team of individuals named "Programmers." These people found a way of taking a specific level of electric voltage and converting it into a "binary code" consisting of "zero" and "one," representing a "yes," or "no" condition, thereby creating the very first and most simple understanding of communication.

Most every child's first word is "Mama" but is quickly followed by "NO." So, simplicity being genius, the simple becomes the complex and a set of "yes" "No" instructions began the art of getting a device to perform a task.

When you tell a child to jump, without explaining what the word jump means, you demonstrate to it what you mean by "jumping." By imitation, the brain records this memory and whenever it is asked to jump it can repeat this performance.

When you ask a computer to jump, it will respond by a prompt stating "This does not compute" because you have not "programmed" it to know what jump means, what direction you want it to jump, how high you want it to jump, how far you want it to jump, or anything else that becomes needed in order to comply with the command. Modern computers that have been developed into android like robotic devices can be told to jump.

Desk models used in a business for processing of tasks associated with normal word processing would not be asked to perform this function. (But it would be pretty cool, to have an android robotic desktop computer that was voice activated and you "told" it to jump off the desk, and it did!!)

As these sets of programs developed, they accumulated these instructions and formed "files" of data. The first of these were the driving force behind each device and its functions, they were aptly named "Device drivers", which, specifically describes this software function. Each device has its own set of instructions, mouse drivers, keyboard drivers and monitor drivers, just to name a few.

As more modern "computing" methods developed instead of referring to files, or typing in commands, images we call Icons were created and you merely had to "Point" and "Click" on these icons to generate the execution of a command, or perform a task. This command generates an electric signal to the computer's central processing unit (CPU) which executes this command based on the memory given to it by its programming. These memories are stored in CHIP(s) (an acronym for "Circuit highway in plastic") that are microscopic in size. These are referred to as microchips.

Basically, all a computer is; is a device that stores and processes saved memories. Based on the functionality of the human brain before, during, and after, birth, it has been storing memories and processing them on a daily basis. Some scientists have speculated that even after death, these electronic signals still exist. These instructions are permanent memory unless and/or until, they are deleted. Software once installed into the permanent memories of the computers main storage unit called the Hard Drive, (named this because it is made out of a rigid disk of aluminum, coated with a magnetic substrate.) will continue to program these various devices, based on the set of instructions that have been loaded into it.

These instructions are titled "Operating System" software or "O/S." Some examples of this are; Windows 95, or Windows 98, or the more popular one, Windows XP professional, and the newer Microsoft products known as Vista and Windows 7,which is a single stand-alone operating system for a new user. NOS, or network operating systems such as Windows Server 2003, and the more up to date Windows 2008, are used to provide multiple users sharing of multiple databases and becomes far more complex and elaborate than their simple predecessors.

I am sure you have all at one time or another heard the phrase "How do you do". The usual response is "fine thank you" or something to that effect. However, when referring to the high-tech industry, how you do something can in fact mean a great deal more. To simplify the ever-growing need for more complex instructions, this book is dedicated to simplicity.

The procedure(s) of doing any one particular task with a computer using any number of programs or operating systems such as in the case of Microsoft Windows Server or workstation is anything but simple.

To the untrained individual who is attempting to understand this somewhat complicated system or to the student sitting in a classroom reading the hundreds of textbooks that have been written on the subject, they realize it is by no means an easy process. For anyone attempting to be certified by Microsoft as a Networking Engineer, they too realize there is a great deal to understand and the sheer volume of it makes most people cringe. It is the intention of this simple outline that you may find the understanding of this complex subject a sweet pill to swallow.

The ABC's of computing and the use of a Windows Server and or professional workstation should prove to be an invaluable source for any user, technician or student. It is a quick reference guide and an excellent training tool. Using the simple set of "keystroke" instructions, along with the brief outline of usage, should make computer usage through the Windows family a whole lot easier.